MW00364792

Teach Your Cat
WELSH

This looks like a really nice, fun way to start learning Welsh – great book!

DEREK BROCKWAY

So, now I have to teach the cat Welsh so that she'll know when the dog is swearing at her? When will this madness end?

LUCY GANNON

Anne Cakebread not only has the best name in the Universe, she has also come up with a brilliantly fun book.

RICHARD HERRING

We don't have a cat or a dog but the whole family love these books (especially the youngsters) and we use them to test anyone who wants to learn, so the next version needs to be... *Teach Your Dad Welsh*!

BETHAN ELFYN

Teach Your Cat

WELSH

Anne Cakebread

Thank you to:
Helen, Marcie, Frieda and Lily, my family,
friends and neighbours in St Dogmaels for
all their support and encouragement.
Gareth Evans, Richard Vale, Siân Melangell
Dafydd, Carolyn and Meleri at Y Lolfa,
Nia and Sophie at The Coach House for
Welsh translations and pronunciations.
And also to Chanel, Coco & Charlie the cats.
Diolch.

First impression 2019
Second impression 2021

© Anne Cakebread & Y Lolfa Cyf., 2019

Illustrations and design by Anne Cakebread

ISBN: 978-1-912-631-08-7

Published and printed in Wales on paper from well-maintained
forests by Y Lolfa Cyf., Talybont, Ceredigion SY24 5HE
e-mail ylolfa@ylolfa.com
website www.ylolfa.com
tel 01970 832 304

I grew up only speaking English.
When I moved to west Wales, I adopted Frieda,
a rescue whippet, who would only obey
Welsh commands.
Slowly, whilst dealing with Frieda, I realised that I was
overcoming my nerves about speaking Welsh aloud,
and my Welsh was improving as a result
– this gave me the idea of creating a series of books
to help others learn.
You don't even have to go abroad to practise.
If you haven't got a cat, any pet or soft toy will do:
just have fun learning and speaking a new language.

– Anne Cakebread

"Hello"

"Shwmae"

pron:
"Shoe-my"

"Come here"

"Dere 'ma"

pron:

"Dare-e ma"

'e'
as in
'met'

'a'
as in
'man'

"Leave it!"

"Gad hi!"

pron:
"Gaad he!"

"Don't!"

"Paid!"

pron:
"Pied!"

"No!"

"Na!"

pron:
"Nah!"

"Very good"

"Da iawn"

pron:
"Dah y<u>ou</u>n"

'ou'
as in
'l<u>ou</u>d'

"How much is it?"

"Faint yw hi?"

pron:

"Vine-t ew he?"

"Don't scratch"

"Paid â chrafu"

pron:
"Pied ah <u>ch</u>rav-ee"

'ch'
as in
'Lo<u>ch</u>
Ness'

"Are you OK?"

"Wyt ti'n iawn?"

pron:
"Ooeet teen youn?"

'ou'
as in
'loud'

"Bedtime"

"Amser gwely"

pron:
"Am-ser gwell-ee"

"Goodnight"

"Nos da"

pron:
"Nohs dah"

"Quiet!"

"Byddwch yn dawel!"

pron:

"Buthooch un dowel!"

'th' as in '**th**is'

'oo' as in 'b**oo**k'

'ch' as in 'Lo**ch** Ness'

'owel' as in 't**owel**'

"Good morning"

"Bore da"

pron:
"Boreh dah"

"What's the time?"

"Faint o'r gloch yw hi?"

pron:

"Vine-t or glo<u>ch</u> ew he?"

'ch' as in 'Lo<u>ch</u> Ness'

"Lunchtime"

"Amser cinio"

pron:

"Am-ser kiny<u>o</u>"

'o'
as in
'g<u>o</u>t'

"Are you full?"

"Wyt ti'n llawn?"

pron:

"Ooeet teen
<u>ll</u>-<u>ou</u>-n?"

Put your tongue on your gums behind your teeth and blow

'ou' as in '<u>loud</u>'

"All gone"

"Wedi mynd"

pron:

"Wedee <u>min</u>-d"

'min'
as in
'<u>mint</u>'

"It's warm"

"Mae'n dwym"

pron:
"Mine do-eem"

"It's snowing"

"Mae'n bwrw eira"

pron:
"Mine boo-roo ey-ra"

"It's cold"

"Mae'n oer"

pron:
"Mine oy-rr"

"It's hot"

"Mae'n boeth"

pron:
"Mine boy-<u>th</u>"

'th'
as in
'<u>thin</u>'

"It's raining"

"Mae'n bwrw glaw"

pron:
"Mine boo-roo gl-ou"

'ou'
as in
'loud'

"It's windy"

"Mae'n wyntog"

pron:
"Mine win-tog"

"It's sunny"

"Mae'n heulog"

pron:
"Mine hay-log"

"Come down"

"Dere i lawr"

pron:

"Dare-e̱ ee lou̱-rr"

'e'
as in
'me̱t'

'ou'
as in
'lou̱d'

"Do you want to play?"

"Wyt ti mo'yn chwarae?"

pron:

"Ooeet tee moyn <u>ch</u>wa-rr-eye?"

'ch' as in '<u>Loch</u> Ness'

"Football"

"Pêl-droed"

pron:
"Pehl-droid"

"What have you got?"

"Beth sy gyda ti?"

pron:
"Beh-_th_ sea guhda tee?"

'th' as in '_thin_'

"Where are you going?"

"Ble wyt
ti'n mynd?"

pron:

"Bleh ooeet
teen <u>min</u>-d?"

'min'
as in
'<u>mint</u>'

"What have
you been doing?"

"Beth wyt ti
wedi bod
yn wneud?"

pron:

"Beh-<u>th</u> ooeet tee
wedee boh-d un
<u>oo</u>-neighed?"

'th'
as in
'<u>thin</u>'

'oo'
as in
'b<u>oo</u>k'

"Headache"

"Pen tost"

pron:
"Pen tost"

'ost'
as in
'lost

"Have you got tummy ache?"

"Oes bola tost gyda ti?"

pron:

"Oiss bohl-a tost guhda tee?"

'ost' as in 'lost'

'a' as in 'man'

"Have you got a cold?"

"Oes annwyd gyda ti?"

pron:
"Oiss ann-wid guhda tee?"

"Where are you?"

"Ble wyt ti?"

pron:
"Bleh ooeet tee?"

"Don't be afraid"

"Paid â bod ofn"

pron:
"Pied ah boh-d of-n"

"Get out!"

"Mas!"

pron:
"M-ah-s!"

"Is that your favourite toy?"

"Ai dyna dy hoff degan di?"

pron:

"Eye duh-na duh hoh-ff deh-gan dee?"

'a'
as in
'man'

"Do you
want a cuddle?"

"Wyt ti
mo'yn cwtsh?"

pron:

"Ooeet tee
moyn c<u>oo</u>tch?"

'oo'
as in
'b<u>oo</u>k'

"Cheers!"

"Iechyd da!"

pron:

"Yeah-<u>ch</u>id dah!"

'ch'
as in
'Lo<u>ch</u>
Ness'

"I love you"

"Dwi'n dy garu di"

pron:
"Dween duh gary dee"

"Happy Birthday"

"Pen-blwydd Hapus"

pron:
"Pen-bloo-ee<u>th</u> Hap-iss"

'th'
as in
'<u>th</u>is'

"Good luck"

"Pob lwc"

pron:
"Pohb look"

"Merry Christmas"

"Nadolig Llawen"

pron:

"Na-doll-ig Ll-ou-en"

Put your tongue on your gums behind your teeth and blow

'ou' as in 'loud'

"Happy New Year!"

"Blwyddyn
Newydd Dda!"

pron:

"Bloo-ee<u>th</u>-in
Neh-wi<u>th</u>
<u>Th</u>ah!"

'th'
as in
'<u>th</u>is'

"Thank you"

"Diolch"

pron:
"Dee-ol*ch*"

'ch'
as in
'Lo*ch*
Ness'

"How many?"

"Sawl un?"

pron:
"Sow-l een?"

1
"one"

"un"

pron:

"een"

2
"two"

"dau"

pron:

"dye"

3
"three"
"tri"
pron:
"tree"

4
"four"
"pedwar"
pron:
"ped-wahr"

5
"five"

"**pump**"

pron:
"pimp"

6
"six"

"**chwech**"

pron:
"chwehch"

'ch' as in '*Loch Ness*'

9
"nine"
"naw"
pron:
"now"

10
"ten"

"deg"

pron:
"deh-g"

20

“twenty”

“ugain”

pron:

“ee-g-*<u>ine</u>*”

‘ine’ as in ‘m<u>ine</u>’

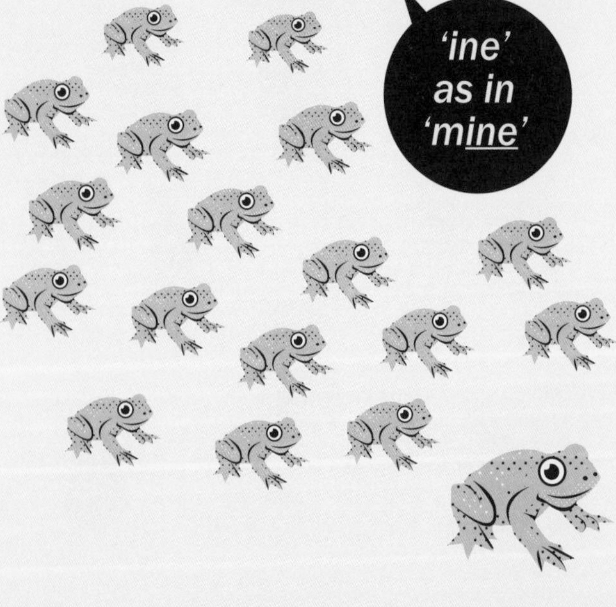

"Are you happy?"

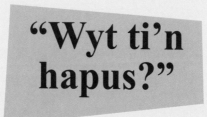

"Wyt ti'n hapus?"

pron:

"Ooeet teen hap-iss?"

"Have you got enough room?"

"Oes digon o le gyda ti?"

pron:

"Oiss digon o leh guhda tee?"

'o'
as in
'h<u>o</u>t'

"Goodbye"

"Hwyl"

pron:
"Hoo-eel"